THE BOOK ON NETWORK MARKETING
SECOND EDITION

D1096956

THE BOOK ON NETWORK MARKETING

TABLE OF CONTENTS

FORWARD

It was exactly 15 years ago that I wrote this book. Carol and I were living in the Bahamas, where she was getting treatment for cancer. While it is so difficult for me to say this, she passed away six years ago. Carol was my inspiration; she was my life. Whatever my achievements were in my life were directly linked to her. We had 35 years of the most beautiful life, anyone could ask for. Thanks to this industry called Multi Level Marketing, or Network Marketing, I was able to be with Carol 24/7 without once worrying about if I could afford to. I will always miss you Carol. You were one in a million.

I could never imagine being with someone else. Let alone marrying again. Yet two years after Carol's passing I met and married Lizanne, a wonderful, beautiful woman with a heart of gold, and always a smile on her face. I am so fortunate to have found love twice. Lizanne has two wonderful daughters; Jennifer, who is a freshman at George Washington University, and Morgan who is a sophomore in high school.

When I wrote this book 15 years ago I had one grandchild, David. Today I have 8 grandchildren. Emily, Jessica, Cameron, Daniel, Caroline, Melanie, and Andrew.

While there have been a lot of changes in my life, the one constant is the personal freedom I've gained through Network Marketing. I've never had to "not do" something because I had a J.O.B. to go to. I have all the personal freedom in my life to do whatever I want, whenever I want. Not only has Network Marketing given me my freedom, it has allowed me to achieve my financial goals beyond what I ever imagined. Network Marketing can give you that constant freedom too. If you work diligently, and consistently and follow the principles in this book, you can achieve personal freedom and wealth. It is exactly what I did to build my organization, which to this day, 20 years later, still pays me.

Let this book guide you on your path as a constant companion. Couple the techniques in here with the new business tools available on the Internet, such as lead generation services, email and videomail products. I can only imagine what those tools would have allowed me to gain had I had them while I was building! I certainly use them now to maintain my connections.

So work hard knowing you are working hard for you. Be steady. Be consistent. Some days will be bad. But the good days will follow. That is the world of Network Marketing. I wish you much success on your journey.

I. Introduction to Network Marketing

I'm about to write the shortest and most concise book on Network Marketing that I can. In 1984 I wrote a book called The First Million is the Easiest, which was the story of Carol's and my success in Network Marketing. This book will be strictly on the nuts and bolts of Network Marketing.

Many people have told me during my years in this industry (which I consider the greatest industry in the world, bar none, provided you have the right product and the right company behind you) that they have never met anyone like me. That observation has come from people earning over one million dollars a year. I don't mean to sound like I'm bragging, but I know my accomplishments have been dramatic. I have earned over $100,000 dollars a month in some programs. Carol and I brought five companies to the top, only to have four of them take it away from us, for one reason or another (either greed, under capitalization, bad management, or all of the above).

I was prospected into this industry eight years ago just like each and every one of you reading this book. The contact comes from a friend, a total stranger, or through an advertisement in the opportunity section of your local newspaper. That's the only way you get into Network Marketing. There is no listing in the yellow pages. You may not know it, but the person that prospected you into this industry may turn out to be the best friend you'll ever have. He or she may have turned you on to the best business venture of your life. What you do with it is another story. I always say opportunity is more than being at the right place at the right time. It's being there at the right time in your life, when you're ready for it, ready to put your blinders on and go through brick walls for it. That means doing whatever it takes, as long as it's ethical and moral. Someone once said, "Help enough people get what they want out of life, and you'll get what you want." Carol and I have changed the lifestyles of hundreds of people. And that's the key to this business. The more you help the people you bring into the business become successful, the more successful you become. You only wish you sponsor someone into your business who becomes more successful than you. And as you may have noticed, I said "your" business. You are the president of your own company. You're the CEO. In the corporate world there's jealousy and politics involved. Not so in Network Marketing. It's a people business. PEOPLE HELPING PEOPLE. You are in business for yourself, but not by yourself.

Although Network Marketing doesn't have many of the negatives associated with the corporate world, it is very much "big business." There aren't too many corporate executives in America who earn the income Carol and I do. And we don't have one employee. Not one. We have no overhead, except a telephone. That's why it's so easy to move our business back and forth from New York to Florida. There's nothing to move. Just Carol and me. No records, no books. The company does the bookkeeping for us. We work right out of our home. It's almost too good to be true, but it is true.

The reason most people don't treat it like a big business is because it doesn't cost $50,000 or $100,000 or $500,000 to get in. They don't have to pay their attorney $5,000 or $10,000. They don't have to sign an 8-10 year lease. They don't have to stock the store with $50,000 dollars worth of product. You see, in Network Marketing the cost is usually about $25.00 dollars to put you on the computer and get the company manual. Then you may order the company's products at wholesale. Your first order is for you to use and share with your friends and relatives. You have to become familiar with your products.

Let's start from the beginning. You've been invited by someone to a meeting, or you have answered an ad in your local newspaper. You're now at your very first meeting. You may see one person at that meeting or 5, 25, 50, 100, or more. But you're there. You're looking around, waiting for the meeting to start. You might be saying to yourself, what have I gotten myself into? I really just came here to get my friend off my back. You see people smiling all around you. Everyone is happy. It appears to you to be the beginning of revival meeting. These people should look happy. Some of them may be making more money in a month than it usually took them two years to make. Sounds crazy doesn't it?

I always laugh to myself when someone says to me at the meeting I'm giving, "Richard, please do this meeting extra good because I've brought someone this evening who's earning over $50,000 a year" when I'm making more than that each month. "You know, Rich, he's a professional." And I say to myself, yes, just like the professional I used to be, getting up the same time every morning, shaving the same time every morning, having breakfast the same time. Then getting to work the same time, having lunch the same time, having dinner the same time, watching the news the same time, going to bed the same time. Boring isn't it? It's what is called the 40-Year Plan. That means most people know what they want to do by the time they're twenty-five, and for the next forty years they go back and forth, and back and forth to a job (J.O.B.-Journey of the BROKE). Back and forth and back and forth. No one ever gets anywhere in life working for someone else. They pay you just enough to keep you there. You get caught up in that security blanket. Just take a good look at the people where you work tomorrow. People who are in the same job situation as you but have been there five years longer than you. Are they living better than you? Are they driving a nicer car than you? Or are they complaining about the same things you are? Well, that's what you have to look forward to. For most people life is just a rut.

Let's get back to that first meeting. There are usually a couple of people conducting the meeting. If it's a husband and wife team, the wife usually does the product part of the meeting, and the husband the opportunity part. A general meeting should not take longer than 45 minutes to one hour. The sole purpose of the meeting is just to introduce the company, product, and opportunity. Plain and simple. Of course, the person or people giving the meeting might make all the difference in the world as to whether you join or not. However, it shouldn't. If the people giving the meeting are really sharp, you may feel you can't duplicate them. It really doesn't matter. What you should be most concerned about are the products and the company they are representing. I've seen some of the most inexperienced people give meeting, and heard the new person say, "If they can do it, so can I." Let's face it, if a novice salesperson were selling me a new Rolls Royce for $50,000 dollars, I'd buy it sight unseen, just because I recognize the value. And that's just how I feel about Network Marketing. I feel like I'm trying to give gold away for nothing.

At your first meeting, your goals might be a couple of hundred extra dollars a month, or $1,000 or $10,000. You might be thinking of working it part time or be ready to jump in full time. I don't recommend anyone quit his or her job to go full time. One of the benefits in this business is that you can start part time and when your income is greater than your full time business, then you can think about going full time. You do it at your own pace. You don't work for anyone. You're your own boss. Whatever it is you're looking for, it's there. You may not see it right now, but it's there. Some of you may think you can never earn more than $1,000 or $5,000 or $10,000 dollars a month part time. And the chances are you're right. If you don't think you can, you never will. I spoke to a woman last week from Kansas City. She cleans other people's homes for a living. She's in our business 4 months and already has made over $5,000 dollars and next month should be making over $8,000 dollars a month. Now that's exciting. And she tells me she doesn't know how she's doing it. She says "I'm just excited about the products, and I share them with everyone."

That's what we all do every day of our lives. We see a movie, go to a restaurant, buy a product we like and then tell our family and friends. And who makes all the money? The manufacturer and then the multitude of people in between. Are we compensated for our recommendation?

No! In Network Marketing, product goes from the manufacturer to the company to you, the distributor. That's how the company can afford to pay out about 50-60 percent to their sales force. There's no middlemen. No retail stores. No advertising. It's all word of mouth.

Each and every one of us is involved with this type of marketing every day of our lives, and we are not even aware of it. The best analogy I can give is as follows: John and Mary are at a PTA meeting. The meeting is over and everyone is looking for a place to go and have some refreshments and talk. John and Mary recommend the new XYZ restaurant that just opened up on Smith Street in the heart of town. Unbeknownst to everyone, the owners of the XYZ restaurant set up a computer and as John and Mary come in with this crowd of people, they give them an identification number. Let's just say the number assigned to them is number 1. Bill and Betty are number 2, Bob and Jean number 3, etc. Let's just say that the next day John has an appointment with a client of his we'll call Tom Watson. And John says to Tom, "Instead of meeting at the ABC restaurant like we usually do, let's meet at the XYZ restaurant. I was there last night with a group of people. The food was excellent, the service was great, and the prices were more than reasonable". So they agree to meet at the XYZ restaurant. Well, imagine the next day Tom has an appointment with a client of his, and because he liked the restaurant, he brings his client there and so on and so on. Well, further imagine that at the end of the year the two owners of the XYZ restaurant say something as follows: "Pete, do you remember that day John and Mary came into our restaurant? Well, because of them and the people they brought and the people they brought etc. etc. etc., we did $320,432.18 worth of business directly or indirectly attributed to them. Let's send them a check for $32,000 dollars." Well, we all know that doesn't happen. As a matter of fact, if John and Mary go to that restaurant and it's busy, they wait in line just like everyone else. Whatever the check comes to is exactly what they pay, and the chances are the owners don't even know who John and Mary are. Yet they were directly responsible for over $320,000 dollars worth of business. Do you get the idea?

That's all Network Marketing is about. Using a product or products and sharing them and the business opportunity with your friends and family. Period.

Some of your friends will say yes to the product and/or opportunity. Some will say no. Some will say no to the opportunity but want to be a customer. Then maybe three months down the road when they realize how good the products are, they may call and ask to become a distributor. You never know. It's strictly a numbers game. I have always said if you can turn yourself into a robot for 60-90 days and do the same thing over and over you will be successful in Network Marketing. Why? Because a robot doesn't know what rejection is.

One of the roadblocks in Network Marketing is rejection; rejection from some of the people closest to you. That includes mothers and fathers, sisters and brothers, aunts and uncles, nieces and nephews. You got it. All of them. You see, they know you best. And especially if you're a dreamer, they say "What's he or she into this time?"

You know, it's funny, but people are so quick to poke fun. But if you hit it big in life, everyone wants in on the action. When you really make it big, everyone wears the clothes you wear, eats in the restaurants you eat in. You could have failed at 20 business ventures in a row, but once you hit it big, "Boy, that guy Jim, he's a genius." So as I said, they may not get in, but they are all watching you. If you give up because you can't get them to join your organization, then they'll all say, "I knew it wouldn't work. Thank goodness we didn't get into that one. I knew I was right honey." But if you keep at it, all of a sudden after 2-3-4 months you start to get some phone calls. "Hi, this is your Uncle John. Are you still in that thing? You are? I'd like to drop by and talk to you about it." Uncle John's priorities might have changed. He may be in need of some extra money. The timing is now right for him. And that's what it's all about. TIMING. Being at the right place at the right time. As I said earlier, what you do about it is another story. Every one of us has that sleeping giant inside of us. Every one of us. For most of us it never comes out. I know hundreds of people in Network Marketing where it came out

BIG TIME. It changed their lives. Both financially and spiritually.

Let's get back to that first meeting. The meeting is now over. Usually your sponsor, the person who brought you to the meeting, is sitting with you. He or she is going to ask you if you are ready to sign up to become a distributor. The next thing you'll probably do is go for coffee and sign the distributor application and order product (usually a couple of hundred dollars worth). But the next step is the most important. That's making a list of everyone you know. And I do mean everyone. Then start inviting them to your home for a meeting on a specified date agreed to by you and your sponsor. One of the great things about this business is that your sponsor or his sponsor is going to do the meeting. Your responsibility at this point is just to invite people and have some coffee brewing. (Never, ever liquor.) Coffee and tea, plain and simple. Don't overdo it. You don't want to make a fancy spread, because although you may be able to afford it, someone else may say to themselves "I can't afford to do this." That could be the one thing that keeps them from coming into your business. Remember, whatever you do will be duplicated by the people you sponsor. If your home is too small or you don't want to have it there, for whatever reason, you can always bring your future prospects to what is called an open weekly meeting, just like the one you attended.

Now, the phone call invitation should sound something as follow: "Hi Bill, this John (with excitement). Mary and I just started a new business venture that we're really excited about. I can't promise you anything, but I would like you take a look at it. (If Bill is married, invite his wife also.) We are having some partners of ours over Tuesday at 8PM to explain it, and I would like you to be there." Bill: "What's it all about?" John: "Bill, it's too important to discuss over the phone. But it's important that you be there." If you have any credibility with Bill, he'll be there. And I might mention at this point, the first meeting you have is usually what separates the men from the boys or the women from the girls. All our lives, we've invited our friends, immediate family and relatives over to our home for dinner or whatever, and they come. Now for the very first time in your life you may experience a feeling that you've never had to deal with before. Not only do some of them not come, some don't even give you the courtesy of a phone call. And that hurts. But you can't take it personally. Just call and invite everyone you know.

Carol and I invited people we hadn't seen in twenty years to our first meeting. We called old friends, friends from grade school, distant relatives who we hadn't seen in years. In a later program, the timing was right with one distant relative who we had seen maybe twice in the last twenty years. He joined our organization and earned over $500,000 dollars in 18 months. The company also paid us about $275,000 dollars in bonuses on the volume he created. Yet I didn't want to make the initial phone call! Carol insisted upon it. It would have been a terrible injustice to both of us if I hadn't made that call. And that's a valuable lesson to be learned.

Some people who are new to Network Marketing don't want to get their friends involved. They feel like they're asking them to buy something, or do them a favor. Imagine that I were a good friend of yours and you got involved with a company we'll call the David Alexander company. You don't share the opportunity with me because you feel you are imposing on my friendship, and then two months later you find out I am in the program, sponsored through someone else. First of all I might be a little hurt with you because you didn't think enough of me to share the opportunity with me. Never prejudge people. And second, let me tell you what you might have missed out on by not sponsoring me. My sponsor in a particular program earned $486,000 on our efforts in a 4-month period, and over $1,000,000 in 12 months. I'm going to repeat that. In one particular program my sponsor earned $486,000.00 in a 4-month period on our efforts and over $1,000,000.00 in one year!

You owe it to everyone you know to tell them about the new opportunity you're involved in. I heard Carol on the phone one day inviting people over that we hadn't seen in eight years. I said, "What are you inviting them for?" They probably had a combined income of over $200,000 a year, and that was seven years ago. What would they need with extra income? However, they did join us and went on to earn $300,000. You never know what stage of life people are in when you invite them to hear about an opportunity. The woman I just mentioned later quit her job as a full time realtor and went full time into our businesses.

You never know who's going to do the business. You may have a good idea, but you never know. Some of the people you would bet your life on do nothing, and some who you think will do nothing turn out to be tigers. And you may sponsor a zero who leads you straight to a tiger. You never know. I once sponsored someone in Boston who sponsored someone in Florida, who sponsored someone in Texas, who sponsored someone also in Texas through an ad in the newspaper. The person I sponsored and all the rest eventually dropped out of the program. The person in Texas, who came through someone who answered the ad, really did something with the program. He went from almost having his car repossessed to earning over $15,000 a month. And that was after four months in the business. Because I sponsored that first person in Boston, we have earned a fortune in the past two years. You never know where it will come from.

Like I said earlier, I'm talking about big business. My accountant once said to me, "You know, Richard, I have clients who employ 400-500 people, have expenses of over a million dollars a month, and don't net what you and Carol do. And you and Carol work right out of your home, and have no employees." Then he scratched his head. Yet he's not in our business. Maybe one day he will be. Maybe one day when the timing is right. This business, just like every other business, is not for everyone.

Who do you sponsor into your business???? That's the $64,000 question. There are some who will say sponsor anyone who passes the mirror test. That means hold a mirror under their nose, and if it looks like they are breathing, sponsor them. Some will say use the three foot rule. That means if anyone comes within three feet of you, sponsor them. Carol and I worked that way for over a year when we first got into Network Marketing. As I look back, after all was said and done, it was a waste of our time. The basic rule of thumb in this business is that quality people lead you to quality people, and "eh" people lead you to "eh" people. Now I'm not saying that it's impossible for an "eh" person to lead you to a quality person. I'm just saying it's not the norm. Or really, I should say it's far, far, far, from the norm. Also, sometimes the people you want it for the most, the ones you love, can't see it and you waste precious time always pumping them up. You want it for them more than they want it for themselves. You have to let go. One of the biggest mistakes a person makes coming into Network Marketing, is wasting too much time with the wrong people. Maybe they'll come around in the future. Maybe they won't.

Now, I consider myself an intelligent person. How could I have wasted so much time in my first program? My sponsor (who prospected me at a muffler shop) saw that I was excited about the business and he didn't want to discourage me by telling me I was going after the wrong people. You see, when I came back from my first meeting (3A.M.), I was so excited I woke up Carol and said to her "I'm going to save the world." Actually it was my first rally. (That's a big meeting where someone in the organization comes in from out of town, someone who is making a lot of money in the business.) When I first started, I went to all the wrong people. That's the mistake most people make. "When I make it big in this business, then I'm going to tell Bill and Jean, Harry, Betty and John, Mark and Sue." Wait until I get those big checks, then they'll believe me." What you have to understand is that you never get those big checks until you sponsor those quality people into the program. Hopefully you go to them first. Look for someone who is successful already. It doesn't matter what they are successful in. You want someone who is good at what they do. They might not be making big money, but that's probably because they haven't found the right vehicle yet. Look for someone people will follow. Someone who has integrity and someone who is honest. There is someone in the clubhouse here in Boca Raton who cleans shoes and golf clubs. If he came to me with an opportunity, I'd listen. Why? Because he's an exceptional person. He's the first one here in the morning and the last one to leave at night. He doesn't leave at 5P.M. when it's time to leave. He leaves when he gets the job done. No matter how late it is. Everyone respects him and admires him. He just hasn't found the right vehicle yet. If you sponsor someone in your town who is well known and has taken everyone for a financial roller coaster ride, that person is not going to be successful in your business because no one will follow him or her.

I think it's important at this point to let you know how I got sponsored into this industry. Eight years ago I took Carol's car into a muffler shop to have a tiny leak repaired. That day changed my life. As I was paying the bill, the fellow behind the counter asked me if I was making all the money I wanted to make. I said to him, "Yes, I do pretty well." Then he said, "Do you have freedom?" And I said, "What do you mean by freedom?" He said, "Freedom to do whatever you want to do whenever you want to do it." I said, "No one can do whatever they want to do whenever they want to do it." He then looked at me with a little smile on his face and said, "Well, I'm involved in that type of business." Now there is a very, very important point to be made here. The point is that I had an open mind. At that time I was in the real estate and insurance business and doing very well. Very, very well. But I was looking for something, so I didn't say to him, "If you're doing so well and have so much freedom, what are you doing behind the counter, full of grease, in a muffler shop?" As I said, I was looking for something so I was ready to listen. The timing was right for me.

Getting back to the muffler shop, I asked the fellow when the next meeting was and he said he was giving one tonight (Friday night) and tomorrow. I asked him for directions and drove home as quickly as possible. I was excited! It was 4:50P.M. I can remember it like yesterday. Carol was standing at the refrigerator starting to prepare dinner for the children, because at 6:00P.M. friends were coming by to pick us up. We were going, along with two other couples, to see Bette Midler, front row center. We had the tickets about two months. I said to Carol "You're not going to understand this, but we have to go hear about something this evening that sounds too good to be true." Carol said "But we have tickets for tonight. Can we go another night?" I said, "Yes, tomorrow night, but I'd rather go tonight." We gave the tickets away and went that night. We sat there and listened just like you did at your first meeting. I was excited but when the speaker from the muffler shop said what the company was, I almost fell through the floor. I couldn't believe it. All this talk about being rich and we were going to have to sell soap. I said to Carol, "let's go, I've had enough" and Carol said, "Let's wait until they have coffee and we'll slip out unnoticed." As we were leaving, the muffler shop man met us at the door and looked at me square in the face and said "False pride? Status hang up?" And I said, "No, we have to pick up our children." (I was lying, I just wanted out of there.) And to think I gave up tickets to see Bette Midler! Before we left though, he gave us an audiotape entitled "Professionals in Blank" (Blank being the name of the company).

The next day, I listened to the tape and said to Carol "There seems to be more to this than we're seeing." Before we signed up though, Carol and I drove around the country to meet people who were already successful with this company. I was impressed with every one of them. They had something that I didn't and I was jealous. They had freedom to do what they wanted to do whenever they wanted to do it. As much as we wanted it, though, Carol and I failed miserably in that program. One of the reasons was because of the people we were prospecting and the other was because the program was around for 20 years. Everyone had heard about it. One of the secrets in Network Marketing, if you want to call it a secret, is getting in before everyone in the country knows about it.

By our second Network Marketing program Carol and I learned to look for people who want more out of life. We look for people who want more quality time with their children and their loved ones, time to pursue hobbies, travel, and enjoy life. Let's face it, most people work so hard, both men and women, that they don't have time. People either seem to have time or money but not both.

You and the people you sponsor into your group will make it when you fall in love with the products and the company, and then tell your story over and over and over. I only wish I had a magic pill that I could give to each and everyone I sponsor, so they could know what I know about Network Marketing. I wish they could know it instantly. But they can't, and everyone goes through their trials and tribulations. Everyone, some more or less than others. It's the ones that stick around long enough who succeed. The ones who really use the products. The people who really get to know the company and its principals and feel loyalty and commitment are the ones who make it. It's as though you're being tested. Let's see how much they can take. Let's see if they can get through the discouraging part. Then when you've paid your dues, something almost magical happens. It's as if the heavens have opened up for you. All of a sudden, everything seems to be going your way. Everything you touch seems to turn to gold. YOU HAVE TO PAY THE PRICE.

By the second month, you'll know a lot more about the company and its products. You should look at your business the first several months as you would a training program. Would you go back to school for a year (10-20 hours a week) to earn an extra $1,000-$5,000 a month part time? I know a lot of people who do and would. Always remember, if you're working for someone, they are paying you just enough to keep you there. And the chances are you're so hung up on security that you'll be there forever.

When Carol and I sponsor someone, it's like being interviewed for a job on Wall Street. As I said earlier, I treat our business like big business. Before we sign that application with the prospective distributor, we do what is called fact finding in the insurance business. I want to know everything I can about this distributor and what his or her goals are. When we find out what their goals are, we start a plan of action. If his or her goal is to make an extra hundred dollars a month, I'm not going to spend 10 hours a day with them. If they tell me they are really serious about the business, then we do some serious goal setting. One must have goals and plans. You have to know where you're going in life. Could you imagine going to the airport and walking up to the ticket agent and saying "I'd like a ticket, please." The ticket agent says "Where to sir?" And you say, "I don't know, I haven't given it much thought." The ticket agent would say "NEXT." And that's about what I do with people who don't know where they're going in life. "NEXT." I can barely take care of my own life, what makes me think I can help a person if they have no goals in life? But if they do have goals but haven't found the right vehicle to get there, well then I can help them. I thought I was going to change the world when I got into Network Marketing. It was a long hard lesson that cost us a lot of time and money.

If a person can define their goals in life, then we sit down and make a plan. I can remember when I first got into Network Marketing and started doing meetings. One of the things I would say when it came to the opportunity part of the meeting was "I want you to imagine that I have a big bushel of money up here in the front. The bushel is filled with money. As a matter of fact it's filled with $2,000,000.00. You can have any part of it, or all of it, but there's a catch. You can't put it into the bank, you can't lend it out, you can't invest it, you have to just go out and spend it. What would you spend it on?" Well, you wouldn't believe the answers I got sometimes. "I don't know." Or "I really can't think of anything." Or "I don't know, hon, what do you think?" I don't know, no one could ever accumulate that much money." Or "I can't dream that big." But if there were a child in that room he or she would say "I'd get trains, and a bicycle, lots of toys, a trip to Disney Land." They would go on and on. You see, they have dreams. The sad thing is that most people forget their dreams. If adults are dreamers, it's usually mentioned as a criticism. "Boy, that John, he's always dreaming." "Why doesn't he come down to earth?" Thank goodness for people like John or we'd still be in the Stone Age. You've got to have a dream on the tip of your tongue or you're not really living. This country of ours was built on dreams. More about goals and dreams in another chapter.

Back to sponsoring, one of the most often asked questions is "How many people should I sponsor?" I'm assuming you, the reader, are serious about this business. You should sponsor a minimum of 2-3 people into your business the first month. If you can sponsor 2-3 your first month and also help those 2-3 people sponsor 2-3 people their first month, etc. etc, you will have the beginning of a nice group. The object of building a group is not quantity of people, but quality of people. Now I'm not saying "just" sponsor 2-3 people your first month. If you have an exceptionally large sphere of influence, then go for it. Just remember if you have the ability to sponsor 50 people your first month, you will lose a lot of them because you can't spend time with 50 individual people. You'll always hear the pros in this business say you can only work with 5 people at a time. There's a lot of truth to that but there are many people who are able to work with more.

What should you do if someone you sponsor wants to sponsor the same person you're just getting ready to contact? Let them do the sponsoring. That doesn't mean if you both know a mutual group of people you should turn over your whole list. It just means if a situation arises where you have both contacted the same person, rather than create hard feelings, let him or her sponsor that new person. They will be part of your group anyway (although it's always important to be expanding your front line).

Remember, your first couple of months are like a training period. You really don't have that much knowledge. You learn by your mistakes. The average new person in this business has just enough knowledge to get them in trouble. This, then, is a must – don't try to explain your business to anyone on your own. I guarantee the chances are you'll lose that person. It's the first mistake a new person makes. That's why you have upline support to help you. If you are not getting support from your upline (they might be in the business only one day longer than you), call the company and find out whom you can call for help. Even if it's a toll call, call the company! So what if it's going to cost you a couple of dollars to find out where you can get help. This is your business and you have to treat it like a business. Many people, when they get into Network Marketing, have only called the area code they live in and maybe a few other states. When you have a good business going in Network

Marketing, you might be calling all over the country. So get used to making those out-of-state calls. Through Network Marketing Carol and I know people in all 50 states. Don't nickel and dime this business to death, or it will nickel and dime you right out of the business.

Before you start, you should decide how much you're going to invest (and how much time you're going to put in). As far as product is concerned, Carol and I have never expended one penny out of our pockets since we've been in Network Marketing. We charge it (Visa, Master Card) and by the time the bill comes, the product has been sold. What other business can you do that in? So there is very little out of pocket cost. All you really need to begin is some business cards and maybe some stationery.

When contacting people, I like to use the phone. There's a lot more excitement in a telephone call than there is in a letter. "Hi John, I'm so excited that I can't sleep or talk right but I've discovered something that I'd like to talk to you about." "How's Tuesday at 7P.M. or would Thursday at 8P.M. be better? Keep in mind that the purpose of that call is just to make an appointment. Don't try to explain anything over the phone. If your friend asks what it's about, just say, "It's too important to discuss over the phone."

Hey, I know how hard it is to make that first call. Sometimes it's still hard for me, but I know from experience that if I pick up that telephone (sometimes it's awfully heavy) I might be calling the next super star in our organization. The more no's you get, the closer you are to a yes. I know rejection is hard to take. Carol always uses this example, which might be helpful. Think of a waitress in a restaurant. She goes from table to table, asking if anyone would like coffee. Eighteen out of twenty might say no, but does she go back to the owner and say "I can't take it anymore. I'm quitting?" Of course not. Why? Because she doesn't take it personally, and you can't either. People are just saying no to the product or the opportunity, not to you personally.

Do I just retail product in the beginning and then turn my customers into distributors? Do I sell a little product and sponsor a couple of people? Do I first use the product until I believe in it, then sell it, and then try to turn customers into distributors? What do I do??? First of all, let me state right here and now, I didn't get into Network Marketing for the product, I got in for the opportunity, and that's why 99 percent of the people get in. So keep that in mind and approach the majority of the people on your list with the opportunity.

Now let's talk about out-of-state sponsoring. Before I get on a plane and sponsor out of state, I'm darn sure going to be strong in my own back yard first, and that means in my own home state. Too many people start flying all over the country and it proves to be expensive and worthless, especially if they are new to the program. Before you travel any major distance, get yourself a good package of information and possibly a videotape and send that out first. Carol and I have sponsored many people out of state that way and it didn't cost us one penny. We would send out a package C.O.D. with the understanding that if the person didn't sign in, we would return their money promptly. I speak to so many people that spend a small fortune sending out literature. There's no reason for it.

The people out of state then invite their friends over, put the television on with the tape I sent them, and they have their first meeting. Sometimes we would suggest they have a speaker phone there and at an appointed time, Carol and I would call up and answer any questions they had. It saved a lot of time and money, and when the out-of-state people had 30-50 people signed up in their organization, I would make plans to go there and do a meeting. At least I knew I had some real players in the game, people who were generally interested in the products and the opportunity. I ran around plenty in the beginning. We made lots of mistakes. Hopefully you won't make the same mistakes, and if you do, you try and learn from your mistakes. Remember, it's a learning process.

Many people use advertising as a sponsoring tool. My advice on advertising is not to use it until you've exhausted everyone you know. If you don't have credibility with anyone, advertising may be the only way you can go. But in this business, people with no credibility as a rule don't do very well. Now I'm not saying that advertising doesn't work. On the contrary, I've seen a lot of excellent people come into Network Marketing through it. It does take a lot of time, though, screening people, and it can be very expensive.

Cold telephone calling is something I've never done, but I believe it is an excellent way of getting new people. After all, sponsoring is a numbers game. When you think about it, that's the way stockbrokers make their living. One way of making cold calling easier is to do it in a group. If you and two or three other people in your organization can get together once a week for three or four hours, and sit down as a team and go right through your local telephone book and make those calls, it would increase your business tremendously. Make it a game, the one who gets the most no's wins. (That person is making progress towards rejection.) Do whatever it takes. Most people don't like doing the uncomfortable. When you can do the uncomfortable, and teach your group to do the same, your organization will grow in leaps and bounds.

Another way of meeting people is to join organizations. You will meet people you would not ordinarily come in contact with.

Make up a small little package of information and using a mailing list, or the telephone book, send out at least ten to twenty pieces out a week. It's very inexpensive, and if you do it on a steady basis, it will work for you. You must be consistent with whatever you are doing. You can't try it for a day or two. Whatever you decide, do it for thirty days or more, and then look at your results. If one thing is not working as you expected, try another, but stick with it.

Walking up to total strangers is something else I have a hard time doing, but I have met many top-level people in this industry who were prospected this way. As a matter of fact that's how I got in!

II. Meetings

We sit down with the person or couple we are just sponsoring and have them make a list of people they know. We go over what they will say on the phone. Now, let's say we are with them on a Thursday. We'll set up a meeting at their home on Monday, a second meeting on Wednesday, and a third meeting on Saturday. The Wednesday meeting is for those people who were unable to attend Monday. Also, the interested people who were there Monday can come back for two reasons. One is to hear the presentation over again and the other is so that they can bring some of their friends. The Saturday meeting is only for the people who signed up to become distributors. This will be a training meeting. At this meeting we go over the nuts and bolts of the business. At the Monday or Wednesday meeting, Carol and I try to pick out someone who looks aggressive and start the whole process over for them.

Let me explain this further and put it in its simplest form. On Monday, Carol and I are doing a meeting for John and Jane. They invite all their friends to their home. After the meeting I'll say, "Okay everyone, we will be here Wednesday to give the exact same meeting. For those of you who have any questions, Carol and I will be here for the next hour. The next step, for those of you who are interested, is to sign the distributor agreement which we have here tonight and to order product. For those of you who are coming back on Wednesday, bring some of your friends. If they sign up to become distributors, they'll be part of your organization, and you've started your business."

Now on the Monday or Wednesday meeting, Carol and I may have noticed a really sharp couple in the group. We would approach them and say something like this: "Hi Mark and Claudia, why don't you have a meeting at your home and we'll do the exact same meeting for you?" If they agree, Carol and I will set the following Tuesday and Thursday for them. At this point I'll say to John and Jane "You have a really interested couple, Mark and Claudia (Mark and Claudia are considered their first level or personally sponsored.). Carol and I are going to do a meeting for them next Tuesday and Thursday. Now we are going to be back here to do a meeting for you next week on Monday and Wednesday. Some of the people who come to your home on Monday can come to the meeting on Tuesday at Mark and Claudia's home." There will be four meetings that week. It's like setting up satellites, giving a wider choice of evenings and locations. Then everyone comes back Saturday for training. This process goes on and on and on.

When you've outgrown the home, some of you will get together and make plans to hold a meeting one or two nights a week at a local bank, hotel, or wherever you can get enough room to accommodate all these new people. It is fair to ask your distributors to share in the cost of renting these facilities. After all, they are also building their business. One suggestion is to charge distributors $2 or $3 for each meeting and any guests they bring are free of charge.

Although I am known for wearing jogging outfits because they are so comfortable, at a meeting I always wear a suit and tie. I definitely believe the dress code should be suits for men and suits or dresses for women. It's called dress for success, and it is important that your organization looks successful. As I mentioned before, this is big business. If you are going to a big business meeting, you don't dress in slacks or jeans, so give your meetings the importance it deserves. It also creates a good impression for a new distributor to see everyone properly dressed. Everyone owns at least one suit, and believe me, I've met some people in this business who came in with only one suit and now have a wardrobe that's worth more than the home they once owned. If you dress for success, you will feel successful, and if you feel successful, you will be successful.

All meetings should start exactly on time. Every meeting that Carol and I personally do start right on time. Sometimes people will come up to me and say "Richard, would you please wait another ten minutes. I have some very important people coming tonight." Well, I can't bet my life those people are going to show up, and to me the most important people are already there. It's more important to show consideration for those who showed up on time than the ones who are late.

Keep in mind that the meetings are basically for the new person and you might find it boring, having heard it all before, but you should be sitting right there with them. I don't care if you've heard the same meeting a thousand times, you belong in the room, not outside in the hall talking and smoking.

When you are doing the meeting, never, ever take questions form the floor. Never! It will interrupt your meeting and you won't believe some of the questions you'll be asked. At the beginning of the meeting just say that if anyone has any question, they should come to the front of the room after the meeting, and you will be glad to answer them. This way people who have to leave on time can.

Whether you have the meetings in your home or at a Holiday Inn, never set up chairs for as many people as you are expecting. If you are giving the meeting at your home, and you are expecting 18 people, set up chairs for 9 people and keep the rest of the chairs out of the way or against the wall. I don't care if the 18 people signed their name in blood that they would be there, set up for 9. This way, if seven people show up, they don't look around and say to themselves "What did the other 11 people know that I didn't know?" It also makes more of an impression when you have to take out extra chairs. Never tell the people you're inviting how many other people are going to be there. Just say "Please, if you can't come, call me so I can invite someone else in your place." No one wants anyone else to take his or her place! One thing I learned in Network Marketing (and I was a good student) is not to re-invent the wheel. You simply follow the same process over and over and over. I heard Mike Tyson, the heavy weight champion of the world, say one day on HBO "I go into the gym and do the same thing over and over and over.

There will be people who will disappoint you, and people who will surprise you. Don't let that throw you. You are the most important person in your group. As long as you believe in the products and the company, then put your blinders on go for it. How much you believe and how much you want will determine how much you'll be willing to go through. If you're really happy where you are in life, you may not want to put up with so much and will quit. But if you really want the finer things out of life and the time and freedom to be with the people you love, you'll do whatever it takes.

III. How to Build an Organization

Network Marketing is a simple business (notice I said simple, not easy). It is just another way of moving products from the manufacturer to the consumer. The more familiar ways of marketing or selling are retail stores, direct sales, or mail order. In our business, we have a product or product line to sell and we also sponsor other people who will sell the product and sponsor people, who will then do the same, and on and on. It is just a process of duplication.

In theory, if you sponsor five people who sponsor five people who sponsor five people, you will have a total of 156 people including yourself. If each person sells (and/or uses for themselves) $100 worth of product, your group volume will be $15,600, of which you will receive a percentage determined by your company's marketing plan.

As I said, these numbers are strictly theory, it never works out exactly that way. However, you can see that in this way you can greatly duplicate your efforts.

Where the breakdown usually occurs is after you have sponsored your initial group of people. Some people are under the mistaken impression that signing someone up constitutes sponsoring them. It does not. That signed distributor agreement is useless unless that person knows how to duplicate his or her own efforts. That's where your role as sponsor is so crucial to your success. You need to stick like glue to that new distributor for the first few weeks. That's when most people quit. Your major responsibility is now to encourage and teach the person you have brought into the program. However, that person has to be willing to meet you half way.

To have a good idea of just how motivated that new distributor is, I suggest asking these questions. "If I could show you something that could be beneficial to you now and in the future, would you be interested? Could you set aside 10-15 hours a week for this project? Will you attend at least one meeting a week? Will you invite everyone you know to a meeting, which I will give at your home next Wednesday at 8P.M.?" If he or she says yes to these questions, you have a motivated distributor. If they say no to one of them, you have a problem, and it's best you know about it now.

What exactly does it mean to help that new person? Well, first help them make that list of people, jog their memory as they are writing. "Who are your neighbors? Who are the parents of your children's friends? Do you belong to any organizations? Who do you send Christmas cards to?" Next, go over what they will say when they call their friends – or better yet, be there when they make a few calls. Next, either do a meeting for them or let them know where a general meeting will be held. Keep in mind, the "meeting" you do for them can be just a few people sitting around a kitchen table. You want them to have some success quickly so they are encouraged. In general, I recommend staying in close contact with your new distributor until there are four or five people in depth in their line, and at least one "leader" type has emerged. That's building a good foundation.

Not all the people you sponsor will be worth your attention, though. If they are not serious, you will only be wasting your time trying to motivate them. Too often people will sponsor a real go-getter and then abandon them because they are so ambitious they don't appear to need help. Instead they spend all their time pushing someone who says they're interested but doesn't show it. Your time should be spent with that excited, ambitious individual. You'll know him or her by their attitude, and how they follow through. They are positive people. They make a large list and call everyone on that list. They call you all the time for information and to share what's happening. These are the people you work with and when they are building a good strong group, you can then start doing more personal sponsoring yourself.

IV. BONDING

Bonding is perhaps one of the most important activities, once you have established your organization. First of all, you especially want to keep in close contact with your first and second level distributors. Also watch for leaders who begin to emerge on your third level. Treat your second level as though you personally sponsored them so if your first level drops out of the program, you won't lose the second person also.

It's a good idea to get together twice a month with your first level people at someone's home for coffee. This is a good time to discuss their organizations with them and hear if they are experiencing any challenges. It's also an excellent time to talk about goals and dreams. Remember, this is your organization. Try and be creative and think up new ideas to make it fun. They are like family, so treat them as your Network Marketing Family. Whatever you teach your first level to do, they in return will do with their first level.

A simple newsletter is also an excellent way to keep in touch and recognize people in your group. Everyone likes to be recognized for the work they are performing. Don't turn the newsletter into a major project though!

V. SELLING

First of all, you must be a product of your product. You must know from personal experience just how good your product or products are. You must immediately replace the old products you were using with the new ones you are representing. If you are selling "Brand A" and someone comes into your home and sees you using "Brand X" it's going to be awfully hard to ever convince them your product is better! You could be losing a customer and a potential distributor.

Let's talk a little about selling product. You hear people say all the time "I can't sell anything", but actually people are always selling. "Hi Giselle, this is John. You've got to see that new movie. It's unbelievable." Or "Honey, taste the chicken. It's great." "But I don't like chicken, Kay". "This is different, Gary, it's a new recipe from my mother." Or "Sweetheart, let's get married." (That's probably the best selling job of all.)

Probably one of the biggest fears for someone new in this business is trying to sell products, even if it's to people they know well. (That's another reason why it's so important to be with a company that has unique or superior products.) My wife Carol is probably the most non-sales type person I know and when we first entered the business, she found it very difficult to go to a neighbor to sell product. It was degrading to her, which admittedly or not, it is to most new people coming into the business. So she bought some tote trays. That's a tray with eight to ten compartments. She filled each tray up with her favorite products and would drop them off to the neighbors, telling them she was in a new business, and would like them to try the products. She also said she would be by in a couple of days to pick up the tray. Never once did she pick up the tray that she didn't receive an order.

Don't let the retail part of the business scare you. It's a lot of people doing a little. I'd rather have an organization of a thousand people doing $100.00 each, than an organization of hundred people doing $500.00 each. Carol and I have never been big retailers. Oh, there have been months when we've retailed $2,000.00 worth of products, but the majority of that came from reorders. The most important thing you want to remember is to duplicate yourself. J. Paul Getty once said "I would rather have 1% of the efforts of 100 men than 100% of the efforts of myself."

It's important that you get back to your customers at least once a month for reorders. You can also make up some little discount coupons to hand out to your customers which specify that if they buy X amount of product, you gill give them X amount of dollars toward new purchases. Also, if your customers refer friends to you, you will give them coupons toward products. After a while, you can go back to your customer and say "Susan, why don't you become a distributor? You've sold over $500.00 worth of product for me this month." That's an excellent way of getting new distributors. They are selling and they are not even aware of it. You see, if they love the product, they naturally recommend it to their friends. Show them how easy it is to become a distributor and keep the profit themselves. That's called getting them into the business through the back door, so to speak.

I love it whenever I hear a person say "Oh, I can't sell. I'm not a sales person." People sell every day of their lives, especially when they believe in something. Don't make this business hard. It's easy and can be the most fun you've ever had. I spoke to someone the other day who earns about $200,000 a year on his full time job. He was so excited, I had to calm him down. He had just sold $22.75 worth of product. Now you have to understand that he made $6.83 on that sale, but he was so excited because it was the first time in his life that he ever sold an actual product. (His dream is to go full time into the business, and quit his job which was responsible for his having two heart attacks and a case of ulcers over the past seven years.)

Although the majority of people initially find selling a hurdle to get over, some people just love it. Every once in a while, you will sponsor a big retailer who enjoys selling, is happy with the profit they are making, and has no desire to sponsor anyone. Let that person know that sponsoring can be very profitable but then leave them alone. You can push a big retailer right out of the business if you keep nagging about sponsoring. Just appreciate the good job this person is doing and recognize him or her for it.

So to sum up retailing, use the products and share them with everyone you know and don't know. SIMPLE.

VI. TOOLS

Just as a carpenter has tools, we do also, in our industry. They are a very important part of your business. Because Network Marketing is a business that works through word of mouth, and not through traditional advertising (this is why companies can afford to pay out the high bonuses they do), you want to do everything you can to promote your business.

One way of getting customers is to wear buttons extolling your product's virtue, or a cute T-shirt doing the same. Be visible! If you hear someone in a supermarket line say "Gee, I wish I could lose weight" and you have a terrific diet product, don't be afraid to speak up! I remember a woman in a former program who used to prospect right in the supermarkets. She had a shirt on her two year old that said "I lost one hundred pounds on the "X" diet, ask me how I did it." She would tell everyone that was really her husband, he just shrunk so much, he looked like a child. She made it fun and got plenty of customers that way.

This book will also be helpful when you are prospecting since it takes the burden of explanation from your shoulders. Not only does it explain Network Marketing but it is a third party showing the income potential, which is certainly exciting. I suggest making up a package consisting of this book, a video and audio cassette (if your company has them), company brochures and any positive media coverage of your product and company. Give this package to a prospective distributor and tell him or her you'll be by in two days to pick up these things and discuss any questions they may have. If you have five of these packages out at all times, I assure you your business will increase dramatically.

I'd like to make an important point here about sales aids, which is that some organizations really go overboard with them. I'm not talking about the company, I'm talking about the organizations that make up the company. Some people make it a business selling tools and forget what they came into the business for. Although there are some very good sales aids that come from within different organizations, the basic rule of thumb is, let the company be in the sales aid business and you be in the people business.

VII. TERMINOLOGY

At this time I want to briefly go over some of the most frequently used terminology in Network Marketing:

Distributor: That's someone who signs the application and in most cases can now order directly from the company (you will receive a bonus on what they order from the company each month).

Qualification Period: That's a period of time when you must meet certain requirements in order to be paid a larger percentage or be paid on a larger segment of people. The qualification period can be anywhere from one to six months.

Pin Level: In most programs, as you go up the ladder of success, you receive a pin to recognize your accomplishments. The higher the pin level, the higher the bonus structure. It's called recognition, and no one does it better than this industry. Carol and I have been picked up on four different occasions by a Lear jet and flown 5,000 miles each time. It's a real thrill, especially when the pilot and co-pilot are serving you snacks. Company conventions can also be terrifically exciting, especially when 3,000 of your peers are standing up, applauding you.

First level or front line distributors: He or she is the person you personally sponsor into the business.

Second Level: She or he is the person directly sponsored by the people you personally sponsored. So on with third level, fourth level, etc. etc.

First level of achievement: You are promoted from a distributor and could now be called a manager, an executive, a senior partner, a captain, etc. This usually means you are going to earn larger bonuses.

Break away: This is when someone in your organization (someone you personally sponsored or someone they sponsored, etc.) goes through their qualification and does the same as you. They now break away from your circle group but you still are paid a percent of their group volume each month.

Upline: The Person who sponsored you and the person who sponsored them etc.

Downline: The person you sponsored and the people they sponsor etc. (I personally never use the word downline, I find it degrading. I use the word family or organization.)

Roll ups: I can't tell you how many people I've met in Network Marketing who never sponsored a person who did anything with the program but they became successful anyway. One of the great things about Network Marketing is that you may sponsor A who sponsors B who sponsors C who Sponsors D, and no one knows it at the time but "D" is going to be the TIGER. A, B, and C drop out of the program. "D" now rolls up to you, and is considered by most companies personally sponsored to you.

Width or going wide: More people sponsored by you on your first level or front line.

Multi-Level Junkie: Someone who is in more than one program at a time. Stay away from them like the plague. I personally don't know of anyone who has ever been successful in Network Marketing that does more than one program at a time (and I know a lot of people in Network Marketing).

Pyramid: In a pyramid, there is no product sold. In Network Marketing you have a product or products to sell. To me, the corporate world is a pyramid. On the top you have the chairman of the board. Next are all the presidents and vice presidents, and then middle management. All the way at the bottom is the janitor. Well, let me tell you, the chances of the janitor becoming chairman of the board of that company is one in a million or maybe a trillion. In a pyramid, there is room for only one at the top, and room for plenty at the bottom. Network Marketing is like an upside down pyramid. Everyone starts at the bottom and there's plenty of room at the top. Also, you can earn more money then the person who sponsored you into the business. In a pyramid, the person who starts it makes the most money, and no one can pass him or her. Enough about pyramids. I hate the word.

VIII. BENEFITS OF NETWORK MARKETING

You are The BOSS.

You make your own hours.

No Territorial Restrictions. Sponsor wherever you want, and live wherever you want.

Tax advantages. (Talk to your accountant.)

No employees.

No overhead.

No limit on what you earn. Give yourself a raise whenever you want to by sponsoring more people and widening your retail base.

Walk-Away Income. This is one of the very best things about Network Marketing. For unfortunate reasons, I had a chance to find out exactly how wonderful it can be. We had a serious health problem in our family in 1987, and I did not work for nine months. Yet the president of our Network Marketing company said "Just tell me where you want your checks sent. You have built a strong organization and it will always be there for you." Not only did we receive a check each and every month, but it continually got larger (our organization was still working, even if I wasn't). The really incredible part is that our checks each month were what the average American earns in two and a half years!

One day recently I was depositing our bonus check for investment with one of the large brokerage houses and I asked my broker "What if I were working here and the same thing happened? How would it affect my job?" He said to me "They would give you a leave of absence but your clients would be turned over to someone else, so you wouldn't be earning any commissions. One month away from the job would be okay but after that (he made a gesture like he was flicking a fly off the edge of his desk), you're out of here."

I will always be grateful to Network Marketing for the freedom from financial worry I had during those nine months. I also thank the thousands of people in our organization who helped make that possible – and supported us emotionally, as well.

IX. ATTITUDE

BE ENTHUSIASTIC! Nothing but nothing takes the place of enthusiasm. Not even a college education at Yale University.

BE PERSISTENT! About 20 years ago an insurance salesman who was trying to sell me a policy would call me every few weeks. He was a pain in the neck but I admired his persistence. Eventually he called at a time when I needed more insurance and I bought a policy from him. Don't waste time with people that are totally negative but don't take them off your list either. Call back every few weeks and let them know how well things are going for you.

BE CONSISTENT! When you get your game plan together, if you do the same thing over and over, you can't fail. Remember the old saying "Winners never quit and quitters never win."

BE POSITIVE! Don't let negative friends or relatives discourage you. They will try to take your dream ("What makes you think you can do that?" or "Those things never work") but what will they give you in return? Will they offer to send your children to college for you? Will they send you on a cruise around the world?

BE COMMITTED! People today don't seem to know what that word means.

BE PATIENT! It takes several months of consistent effort before you can really tell how much you have accomplished. Think of yourself as a farmer. When a farmer plants his seeds he doesn't get up the next morning expecting a garden. Even with the best sun, the best rain, the best weather conditions, the best soil, and lots of care, some of those seeds will sprout in a week, some in a month and some will never come up. Only time will tell with your people also. Some of your friends are just waiting to see how you do (we call them the "wait and see-ers"). If you stick around long enough, some of them will eventually join you.

X. COMPANY

What if you are doing all the things I've mentioned and you're still not achieving what you expected? You may be with the wrong company.

What kind of company does one look for? That's another $64,000 question. First of all, I would never become a distributor for a company where none of the principals were ever distributors themselves. If none of the principals were ever in the trenches, they can't know what it is you have to go through. There are a lot of companies going into Network Marketing because they know there's a lot of money to be made. Then when the president of the company has to start signing checks to distributors for $5,000, $10,000, $25,000, $50,000, or even $100,000 a month, all of a sudden it doesn't seem right to him. He thinks it's just his products that got the company where it is. It was the distributors, and it will always be the distributors. Find out as much as you can on the background of the principals of the company. You'll save yourself a lot of aggravation and money.

Look for a company that has long range goals. Sometimes that's not so easy to find out. Try to stay away from start up companies. They have no track record. About 95% of them are out of business within six months. Carol and I get prospected by just about every new company that comes out, and most are usually not around in six months. They all say, "This is the hottest thing. This is ground floor opportunity." As Craig, a good friend of mine says, "The only thing wrong with ground floor opportunity is, it never gets off the ground."

The point I'm trying to make is, most companies never last. I can count on one hand the companies that have come out eight years ago and are still around today. The best company is probably one that has been around for at least a year or two. That way you have some idea of stability. Not much but same.

Also check your company's financial standing and, of course, the best situation would be a company that is debt-free.

The company's marketing plan should be fair and equitable but otherwise should not be the determining factor in selecting a company. As I've mentioned often, the company's products are more important. (They should be unique, superior, emotional and consumable.) If you join a company that has inferior products and the most fantastic marketing plan, your experience will be short lived with that company, I promise you. The company can pay out 90% but if the products aren't unique or superior, they will be impossible to sell. 90% of nothing is nothing. I can remember a company that came out with the greatest literature and video tape that I have ever seen in Network Marketing. They had some of the greatest sports figures representing them. They also spent millions of dollars to attract top notch distributors. The only problem was their product was nothing special and the company lasted less than a year.

You should think a hundred times before you join a company that is front loaded. That means that you have to buy X amount of product to reach a level. It's called "buying in." I've never seen one last. When your garage is full of product and you can't fit the car in, that's when you start thinking about what you got yourself into.

Policies and procedures and marketing plans vary from company to company, so the following descriptions are very general.

Any necessary accounting is usually done for you, so you don't have to keep track of everyone's volume and what money they are owed. Most companies send you a computer printout at the time they mail you your bonus check. It's a complete readout of the people you sponsored and the people they sponsored, all the way down to and including the last person sponsored each month in your organization. You would usually get a check somewhere between the 15th and 20th of the following month.

Companies pay a certain percentage on the volume your group produces and that percentage increases as your volume increases. The percentage is often high (10%-25%) because you are spending time helping these people. Once someone you sponsored duplicates your efforts by building his or her own group, they "break away" from you. Now they have earned the right to earn the high percentage on their own organization.

You are still compensated for your efforts on building this group, however. Most companies pay 5% on breakaway group volume each and every month you are active (active is ordering a certain amount, usually $50-$100, in a given month). The number of people you personally sponsor who break away from you usually determines how many levels of breakaways you'll be paid on.

Even though it sounds as though you get paid less by helping someone break away, it actually should be more. As more and more people join that organization, the volume grows larger each month. For instance, their volume when they were part of your group might have been $10,000. Let's say you were earning 12% of their volume. That would mean $1,200 to you. But let's say they have a $40,000 group volume as a breakaway group and you were receiving 5%. That would mean $2,000 to you in bonus money.

Then, of course, there is the retail profit you receive from selling your company's product. That can range anywhere from 20%-50%. You shouldn't be as interested in the retail mark up, though, as how much they are paying you on your organization.

I feel it is most important for a company to have a board of distributors. A company that selects experienced distributors from the field to represent all distributors shows a sensitivity toward the needs of its people. This board should meet on a regular basis and have input as far as challenges that are arising in the field. Since distributors are in the unique position of knowing what sales aids will be helpful, where company support is needed, and what changes are needed in policies and procedures, they should have a voice in some of the decision making. The appointment or election of such a board also demonstrates that the company plans to be around a long time.

One last thing you should look for when considering a company is whether or not you can will your business to your heirs. You don't want to build a big business only to have it revert back to the company should you no longer be here.

XI. CROSS GROUPING

When you signed your application to become a distributor, you signed up with an organization that was directly linked to the company. In other words, if you could follow your family tree all the way up, you would find a person considered first level to the company, with no sponsor. These people are usually referred to as "founders." There could be five, fifty, a hundred different organizations that represent a single company. Many of these leaders run their organizations differently from the others. Where they are all alike is they all purchase the products and literature from the company for the same price, and all get paid the exact same way. Where they differ, though, is their own personal philosophy on how to run an organization. Though this is a business of caring and sharing, sometimes it's not a good idea to go from one organization to another for information. You can become very confused and in some cases feel that the other organization is more adept than yours. It's usually not your organization's fault if you're not doing well, but your own. If you're with a good company, they won't allow you to switch organizations unless you are inactive for six months. However, I've found that if people took all the energy they use to complain about their upline and put it into their business, they would accomplish much more.

XII. NETWORK JUNKIE

I mentioned the "Network Junkie" a while back but I feel it's necessary to devote a special section to this subject because this person can lead you and your group into total destruction.

You yourself could even become a "Junkie" innocently enough. When you join this industry, somehow everyone in the world seems to get your name and address. You start receiving mail from everyone concerning their different programs. A lot of them start out by saying "This will enhance the program you're with now. You really don't have to work it." Well, anything you don't have to work, won't work for you. If you decide you like this program, whatever it is, and bring it into your group, this shows your group that anyone else can bring in what they want to also. Remember, whatever you do, your group will duplicate it. All of a sudden, you'll have an organization which has fifty different programs running through it. Everyone's efforts are now diluted.

If I find a "junkie" at one of my meetings, I very politely let them know they are no longer welcome to attend. You'll recognize him or her by their "Junkie Jacket." It contains about twenty pockets – for the brochures of all the different companies they are in! Just remember, these people could bring your organization down like a building hit by a tornado. They are like vultures ready to pounce on their prey. They can't build an organization on their own so they find an established group and try to infiltrate. They never become successful but in the meantime they wreak havoc on everyone else's efforts.

As for you yourself, you should believe in the program you've chosen with all your heart and soul. Be sure you've done everything possible to make it work before you start looking elsewhere.

XIII. This Is Your Life

And what are you going to do about it?

I'll never forget my first Network Marketing meeting. Before the man from the muffler shop talked about the product and the company, he kind of set the mood with a lot of facts that I found unbelievably interesting. Some of these facts really started me thinking about where I would be in the next twenty years or so. The problem is, we never think we're going to get old, and then it happens just like that. One of the things he said that hit me like a ton of bricks was (and these are real facts put out by the insurance companies) that out of every hundred people born, by the time they reach age sixty five, ONE WILL BE WEALTHY. JUST ONE!!! I forget the exact breakdown, but the rest (the ones that are still alive) will still be working or will be dependent on social security, family and relatives. If only one out of a hundred will be wealthy, will it be you?

The facts also went on to say that the average man at age sixty eight has less money than he did at age eighteen, and that's after fifty years of hard work. I most definitely did not want to become one of these statistics.

As I sat there thinking about all the numbers, I could remember talking to Carol over the past couple of years about our future. "You know, we have three daughters who are going to be going to college and getting married within the next ten years. We're probably looking at $200,000. Where is the money going to come from?" (And I made an excellent living,) Carol would always say "Don't worry about it. My parents did it and their parents did it, and somehow, someway, we'll do it. But I said to Carol "I don't want to be like your parents, and the majority of people, who re-mortgage their house to pay for everything." Well, today our oldest daughter, Robin, has graduated from college and we were able to give her the wedding of her dreams. Laura just completed four years of college, and Jennifer starts her third year of college in the fall. It was all very expensive, but I didn't have to re-mortgage our home to pay for it. It's a nice feeling to know that we had the cash to afford it, and didn't have to spend the rest of our lives paying it off. I don't know of anything else I could have done to pay these huge bills if it were not for Network Marketing. It's nice to be able to go now and pay now, rather than go now and pay later.

XIV. SELF-MOTIVATION

This business requires a great deal of self-motivation. There is no one standing over you, telling you to make that phone call. You have no place to report to each day, no one to make sure you show up for work. There will be no one coming up to you, asking to join your business (at least not in the beginning). All the effort and drive have to come from within you.

Until Network Marketing, I'd spent a lifetime pursuing the "American Dream" fruitlessly. My fantasies were strictly Horatio Alger, and I'd never lost faith in my belief that America offered everybody the chance to achieve their fondest goals if they searched long enough and were willing to work hard enough for this final reward. I'd not been satisfied to settle for anything less and this has been why I'd refused to follow in my Dad's footsteps, as so many of us do. I knew deep inside me that somehow the right time would come, and if I recognized it and seized it and refused to let anything interfere with it, I'd be riding the golden crest at last. I think it was this restlessness, this dissatisfaction, this deepest need to be one of the outstanding achievers in life that bedeviled me and kept my emotions on a constant merry-go-round. I knew I could do it if only the right opportunity came to me. I recognized that here it was finally, and this is what propelled me into the dedication and almost mania that made us so successful at it. Network Marketing. I love it. This, then, is the most important factor I can think of which will also make you a success with Network Marketing. You must have a need, a desire, an almost insatiable yearning for a better way of life.

There were certain specific things that happened in my life that prepared me to accept opportunity when it came my way. These stories from my past will give you an idea of why I wanted to make my life a success (and to me, success is more than accumulating money. It's also being a good husband, father, and friend and being the best person you can be). Before I go all the way back in time, though, I want you to know that when I chose Network Marketing as my vehicle, I had added another motivation:

My friends would always say to me, "Richard, what is it you really want out of life? You have a wonderful wife, great children, a beautiful home, two late model cars, why are you always looking?" And I guess what I wanted, besides health and happiness, was more than one Sunday a week. To me, the greatest day in the week is Sunday. I enjoy having family and friends over, people splashing in the pool, me making hot dogs and hamburgers. I love it. But always around 3:30-4:00, I'd get that pain in my gut that said tomorrow is Monday. Back to the same old job. Back to the same headaches. (People who quit, people who left and took the listings in the office, deals that fell through etc.) It was always problems and more problems. Why couldn't there be more than one Sunday a week? Why couldn't Tuesday be Sunday, or Thursday be Sunday if I wanted it to be? Well, I found what I was looking for in Network Marketing. When I built an organization of independent distributors they would be in business for themselves. If I opted to take a vacation, that didn't mean they would take a vacation. So when I went to that first meeting, I got turned on by all those circles. I understood how I could duplicate my efforts over and over and I knew as soon as I succeeded, any day could be Sunday.

How often I've thought about the factors which led to Carol and me becoming involved with Network Marketing. For Carol the reason are obvious. She needed to feel her husband and daughters could afford financial ease and know a way of life that brought them comfort and peace of mind. Carol had been fortunate enough to live a complacent middle-class existence, and while her luxuries had been limited, she'd certainly never wanted for the really necessary things. Her foremost priorities included a nice home, college educations for the children, proper marriage sendoffs for them, and eventually, a fulfilling and adventurous later life for herself and me.

I was brought up in a family where there was no emphasis on school, so of course, I quit when I was sixteen. My father told me "Don't worry about anything. As long as you have Blue Cross and Blue Shield, you've got everything you'll ever need in life." I started to go to work with my father the summer I was fourteen. My father was the head printer in a factory. Can you imagine being in an environment like that at fourteen? I started full time when I was sixteen. What a future I had.

I can remember like yesterday breaking for lunch. There would be the same fifteen guys sitting around comparing their lunches and then eating. "What, tuna fish again!" Or "Look how much salami my wife gave me. Does she think she's feeding one of the kids?" The same complaints day after day. The same boring conversations too. "Hey, what's on television tonight?" "Did you see Break The Bank last night?" Hey, that Roy Rogers, isn't he something?" "Hey Richard, how are you doing?" "You're a lucky kid, Richard, one day you'll be up there on the press feeding the paper into the machine instead of sweeping the floors and cleaning the ink off the rollers." Not one person ever said to me "What the heck are you doing here? Go back to school or something."

But at sixteen years old, I knew I didn't want this to be my future. I'll never forget one particular day. I had swept the floor, cleaned the ink off the rollers on the press, and loaded the press with stock for the next day's run. I was all done for the day and it was 4:15P.M., fifteen minutes before quitting time. I had taken out a newspaper and started reading the sports section of the paper when my father came up to me and said "Did you sweep the floor?" I said "Yup." "Did you clean the press?" "Yup." Then he said to me, with a look to kill, "Richard, don't ever, ever let the boss see you doing nothing. Not ever." I will never forget that. I said to myself right then and there "I want to be the boss one day. I will never have to look busy when I have finished all my work, no matter what time of the day its."

When I was 13 years old, I was fortunate to work as a caddy that summer. For the first time in my life I saw men come to a golf course everyday and play a round or two of golf. How could they do this? Didn't they work? At first I thought they were probably on vacation, but when I saw them throughout the summer, I figured out that this was a way of life for them. At

13, I was aware enough to figure that out. Most of them had Cadillacs and Lincolns. Whenever I would hitch a ride home, I would only get in a Cadillac or a Lincoln. I'll never forget my first ride in a Cadillac. It was bigger and smelled different than the interior of our family car. The leather smelled wonderful and the seat felt soft and luxurious. The radio sounded richer. I knew right then and there that I would own a Cadillac one day. I got my first one when I was 26 and have never driven anything else since, except my white Rolls Royce. You see, the seeds were planted when I was 13 or so. My subconscious mind kept watering those seeds. I kept nurturing them, I didn't know how I was going to get where I got in life, but I knew one thing, and one thing only, I was going to get there.

If there was one incident in my life that spurred me on and gave me a sense of urgency more than anything else, it's what I call "The Uncle Irv Story." I was honorably discharged from the United States Air Force on Jan. 1, 1965. Carol, Robin (my one and a half year old daughter) and I headed back home to New York. We moved in with Carol's parents (who are the salt of the earth). I promised Carol we wouldn't be there more than a year. (It wound up being exactly 364 days.)

I started in real estate. I had never sold anything in my life, but I was determined to learn because I had nowhere else to turn. I had quit school at sixteen and my only training was printing, which I definitely did not want. Real estate was going to be my vocation. My ambition was to make about $7,500 that first year. I was making $300 a month in the Air Force, so that seemed rather ambitious to me.

One day, Carol, Robin, and I were invited to my cousin's brand new home. My cousins were about five years older than Carol and me. The whole family was invited to this house-warming party. There was a group of aunts and uncles sitting around one of the tables, eating lunch, when one of my uncles asked me what and how I was doing in the business world. I told him I got a job as a real estate salesman and that I hoped to earn $7,500 my first year. With that, my Uncle Irv looked up at me, with a mouth full of food, said "Seventy five hundred? That's nothing! My son-in-law is earning twenty thousand dollars a year as an accountant with NBC." I'll never forget the feeling I had inside me. I was embarrassed in front of Carol, but right then and there, I promised myself that no matter how many long hours and hard work it took, I would earn more money than anyone else in my family. My uncle never knew it, but he was responsible for giving me a spark in my heart that has never gone out. That one thing he said has made me one of the most competitive people I know.

Uncle Irv also said to me "Where are you going without a college education?" He forgot that life can also be an education.

I believe that if we try hard enough we can bring to the surface different things or feelings that have perhaps kept us from attaining all we hoped to. I further believe that if we can concentrate on those feelings when we're all alone, we can not only capture those feelings, but can change them to something positive. Did you ever hear "You'll never be anything" or "You're too lazy" or "You're not smart enough"? We start to believe what we hear, our subconscious mind accepts it, and we become exactly what other people think. If they think we're nothing, we usually become nothing. If you grow up hearing day in and day out "One day you'll be a doctor," chances are one day you'll become a doctor.

When I was twelve years old, I was a little league pitcher. I loved baseball, and I was a very good pitcher. The first year I pitched 13 games, 8 of which were no hitters. That summer my father took me to see my first game in Yankee Stadium. When I saw the pitchers warming up, I couldn't believe a ball could go that fast. Up until then, I thought I was fast, but I was nothing compared to this. I looked up at my father and said "Do you think I'll ever be able to pitch that fast?" He said nothing but gave me a look that said "What, are you dreaming?", and then looked away. If only he would have said to me "For your age, you're faster than anyone of them," he could have given me the confidence I so badly needed. Maybe he hated baseball because he threw his arm out one winter while pitching in spring training for the St. Louis Cardinals. But I believe had my father's answer been different, one day I could have been a major league pitcher.

Sometimes we have to take a look at the ideas we have about ourselves and think about where they came from. An overly critical parent or teacher?

An older sister or brother? Are these "tags" holding you back from achieving your true potential?

Please take some time to think about what motivates you (or doesn't) and why. All of us have life experiences that have led us to where we are now. If you aren't totally happy with where that is, it's not too late to change.

XV. Urgency

When people ask me how I have become as successful as I have in Network Marketing, it always comes back to the same word – "URGENCY." I don't know if most people know what that word means. They may feel it at times throughout their lives, but I don't think most people really understand what it means.

Could you imagine, I mean really imagine, being tied up to a tree with a bomb, powerful enough to level a ten story building, at your feet, ready to go off in five minutes. You're all alone, thirty miles from anywhere and anyone. One minute has gone by and you're trying desperately to free yourself, but you know it's impossible. Two minutes: Your life starts flashing before you, you start thinking of events that you have never thought about before. Three minutes: Your body starts shaking violently, the sweat starts pouring out, your mouth is so dry it becomes hard for you to swallow, and it becomes difficult to breathe. Four minutes: You can hear your heart pounding like you've never heard it before. You look down and your heart actually looks as if it's going to push right through your clothing. It's beating faster and faster. Something is going on in your body that you've never before experienced. Thirty seconds left: Your legs go limp, and the only thing holding you up is the rope around your waist. The ticking of the bomb sounds so loud to your ears now that your head begins to throb unmercifully. Ten seconds left: Everything in your body lets go and it feels as though all your organs are coming unglued. Your tongue becomes so swollen that you can't close your mouth. Five seconds left: You're not even thinking to yourself "Oh, if only I had another chance at life", because you know nothing can save you. Nothing! Three seconds left: You're praying that the bomb will go off, because you can't stand the pain any longer. Two seconds left: A figure stands before you! You don't recognize him but you're asked a question, "If I save you, will you be the very best person you can be? If one day someone prospects you into an industry referred to as Network Marketing, will you give it your best effort, put your blinders on and go for it no matter how much rejection you get? Will you attain the highest level with that company in the shortest amount of time? Do you think you would feel a sense of urgency to escape your present situation? Well I don't need a bomb at my feet to feel that way.

Last night Carol and I had dinner at the home of someone in our organization. At the dinner table the woman asked me "What is the real secret to success in this business?" I looked at her and said "Do you really want to know? It's doing the same thing over and over and over and over." Her husband looked at me and said "It's got to be more than that." I said "You don't want it badly enough." "You don't really have an urgency." These people live in a big, beautiful home. I said "Albert, what would you do if tomorrow you and your wife had to move into a five hundred square foot home, drive a twenty year old car, and never again go to a show, go out to dinner, or have the nicer things in life? What would you do if the only way you could get back your present lifestyle was through Network Marketing?" He said "I'd do whatever it took. I'd work the business twenty-four hours a day." I said, "Now you've got it."

If you are coming into Network Marketing to make an extra couple of hundred dollars a month, that's one thing, but if you're coming in to build a tremendous business, you must expect to give it your all. You must become obsessed with your business. When your friends who are not in the business stop talking to you because of your obsession, that's when you'll know you're on the right track. Could you imagine Ted Williams, in his teen years, dating like the rest of his friends? I'll guarantee he spent every possible moment practicing his sport and if the bat wasn't in his hand, it was in his mind.

If you want to play "Happy Birthday" on your grand piano, it won't take long to learn, but if your ambition is to play the greatest piece ever written, it's going to take years and years of practice. In Network Marketing it might only be months before you start reaping the rewards, but you're going to have to work hard. The rewards are worth it though. Not since I was prospected eight years ago has life been so sweet. If there were no such thing as Network Marketing and I lost every asset I owned, I would rather be six feet under than ever have to go back to a 9-5 routine.

XVI. Goals

By now I am sure you have a good understanding of Network Marketing. If you've stayed with me up to this point, I'm sure you understand just how much I believe in it. It's the only system of selling I know of which offers everyone the opportunity to become rich, and you don't need a college education or extensive training to accomplish this. What you do need, is the ability to withstand any sort of negatives that crop up and a profound personal need for financial security and freedom, or whatever it is you really want.

To help you reach your goals, I strongly suggest reading positive motivational books. They will help your attitude a great deal. I remember the first motivational book I ever read (and still re-read): Think and Grow Rich by Napoleon Hill. It has helped me immensely. One of the most important things it taught me was that you must have a burning desire in order to succeed. I also learned from Hill's "three feet from gold story" that most people quit when success is right around the corner. You must fill your head with a lot of positive ideas day in and day out. There are times you'll need it more than you think.

When I went to my first Network Marketing meeting in 1980, the person from the muffler shop did the bushel basket story. I raised my hand and said I wanted a white Rolls Royce. Carol looked at me and said "You never mentioned that to me." I said "I never thought it was within reach." About a week later I went home and wrote down my plan of action, what I was going to do to get it, how much time I was going to invest, and the date when I would have it. That piece of paper stayed on my night table next to my bed. Every night before I went to bed and every morning when I got up, I read that piece of paper until I had it memorized. It was a two-year commitment. I didn't get the Rolls Royce on the day I had written on the paper, I got it about 5-6 months later. But I got it. And I'll never forget the day Carol and I took a limousine to pick it up. I was so proud. Not so much about the car as I was about completing my goal. Me, owning a Rolls Royce! Me, the only one on both sides of my family that didn't graduate from high school. I was proud! I still get a kick out of driving that car and sometimes watching people almost go off the road while they're doing a double take. What most people don't know is that you can have just about anything in life you want, as long as you think you can and then make a plan of action to reach those goals.

Not only is it important to write down your goals, you must visualize what it is you want. Do you want a new home? If so, go around looking at what you would consider a dream home. How many rooms does it have? How would you decorate it? Or do you want a luxury car? Go to the dealership and take one out for test drive. Smell the leather, listen to the quality of the radio. What color would your car be? Would you love to travel to exotic lands? Go to a travel agency and get some brochures. Imagine yourself walking those splendid beaches or experiencing different cultures.

Whatever your dreams, surround yourself with those reminders. Tape pictures of that car, house, yacht on your refrigerator. Write notes to yourself and put them next to your bed, on your bathroom mirror. Repeat your goals, out loud, the first thing in the morning and the last thing at night. As Napoleon Hill says "You must work yourself into a white heat of passion."

No matter what your current circumstances are, if they satisfy you and you've settled into a complacent niche, even though your job and lifestyle are not what you first set out for, then Network Marketing is not for you. If you've lost that wonderful ability to dream and recapture the fantasies of your childhood, all I can do is wish you well and extend my sincerest hopes your life will in some ways be a happy one. But – and this is a big but – if you're not satisfied because you still hope for more out of life, if you still fantasize about wealth and beautiful lifestyles and the ambitions of your childhood: custom cars, furs, jewels, boats, vacations, everything money can buy, and most importantly, the time and freedom to enjoy them in, then, Network Marketing is for you. If you don't recognize that and you don't get involved with every ounce of energy and enthusiasm and faith you possess, you'll be missing out on the biggest chance you'll ever have to gain all these magical dreams at last.

As I've stated, it doesn't take specialized training or years of educational tutoring. What it does take is this awareness of yourself and your fondest ambitions and desires and the strength of will and determination to say to yourself: here it is and no matter what it takes, I'm not going to accept "no" for an answer. I'm going to do it, no matter what it takes.

XVII. Guidelines

Carol and I use certain guidelines in Network Marketing. To start with, you must believe in the product or products sold through your organization. I think one of the reasons Carol and I failed in our first program, beside it being around for twenty years, was that we were not inspired by their products. Certainly they were a marvelous assortment of household needs, which are constantly in demand, but somehow we could not find in our imaginations or inclinations to respond to these products. It was totally different with us in some other programs. There was something that set off the Fourth of July sparklers in our psyches. We believed in the products with every ounce of our convictions. We were completely obsessed with our faith in the products and the company, so that it became almost a mania with us. This is what I mean about belief in the product. While it isn't necessary to have quite as strong an attraction as we do for the product and the company, there must be a personalized association with the product and the company. Whatever the reason might be, you must truly be convinced this particular product is worth spending every second of your waking day extolling its virtues and convincing others to believe in it as you do. There can be no middle road in this. If you don't have this total faith in the product and a willingness to share this faith regardless of the circumstances, then this particular product is not your vehicle to achieve Network Marketing success with. There are other companies on the market, search them carefully until you find the one every fiber in your being tells you, you must be part of it. And when you do find this company, stay with it.

The second rule, and for many this is the most difficult to keep, is that a logical acceptance of the rejection factor must be built into any kind of sales plan. There will be a large number of people you will approach who will fail to be enthusiastic about the product you represent, or the idea of Network Marketing. You cannot deal with this rejection on a personal level. You must remember at all times, these people are negating the product and/or marketing plan, and it has nothing to do with their acceptance of you. Whatever it takes for you to equate this properly on both an emotional and intellectual level, you must achieve this balance or your enthusiasm will not sustain itself strongly enough to take you over the long haul. If you can see the validity of your product and the worth of Network Marketing, eventually you will find others who will share this belief with you, and the first group of believers will be the start of your own road to riches. We human beings differ on so many levels that it may take what seems forever before you begin to assemble your first firm group, but if you speak to enough people often enough, eventually that group will be formed.

The third rule is determination. Network Marketing success can be yours, but only if you are determined that whatever it takes, no amount of work or meetings or constant telephoning and prodding of prospective members and current members of your group is too much for you to endure. (Speaking of meetings, it is essential you attend them on a regular basis. We never met anyone who created a successful organization without attending meetings on a consistent basis.) You must be the inspiration, the role model by which everyone else patterns themselves. Your enthusiasm must be endless, and your willingness to meet with others and share this enthusiasm must have no time limits or boundaries which hinder your ability to spread the good news. If you keep up this determination, no matter what happens that is perhaps a source of interference, you will eventually find others who become so caught up in the determination you inspire that they, too, will be willing to match your efforts and even surpass them in time.

The fourth rule is organization. You must keep a constantly expanding index file system whereby you are always up-to-date on whom you've approached, what their reactions have been, what people are possible members of your organization, what people are positive prospects, what meetings you've attended, what meetings you've personally hosted, how much product you've personally sold, how much product your group has sold and is currently selling. (Sometimes that's almost impossible to tell because your group is expanding so quickly. You may have to wait for your printout from the company.). In short, you must be able at a moment's notice to put your finger on every aspect of your efforts and the progress or lack of it in any given area. You cannot hope to build a strong first level group if you're not aware of every member of the group and his or her personal progress. This index will be a constantly shifting one at first as certain members of your group fail to live up to their initial enthusiasms and are replaced by new members you've recruited. It may take some time before your first group settles in and performs satisfactorily, and so keeping your index system in tight order may take some doing for a while. But it is the only logical way of keeping track of your progress and theirs, and so it is a highly necessary part of your whole regimen. Never forget your promotion to leadership level entails a strong group of people who have the potential for duplicating your efforts and the ability to sell and keep recruiting. So it is up to you to develop this unit no matter how many times you add, then discard, then add again to your index cards. The same goes for your ledgers which keep track of sales. Know to the penny who has been responsible for what amount so you can maintain a tight control and thereby be ready to encourage and abet any member of your group who seems to be faltering. You are the leader and the manner in which you organize this leadership may very well prove to be the key factor in achieving your successful rise in the Networking Marketing plan.

The fifth rule is awareness. You must keep constantly abreast of any and all changes in the products you represent so that you may include any advances which might enhance the product's viability in your meetings. Know your product and know it well. Be prepared on any occasion to speak about it knowledgeably and in depth so that you can immediately negate any adverse comments which might arise, and even more importantly perhaps, convert a negative reaction to a positive one. You must know what you are talking about regardless of the time it takes to gain this information.

You must be aware of all your product's strongest virtues, and also be prepared to field criticism graciously and knowledgeably so that everyone you meet, both at meetings and every day life, will be able to understand and appreciate why you value your product above other perhaps similar products. So many times, the willingness of the new person to get involved depends on how much they are impressed by those who have already become subscribers. If they buy you and your knowledgeability, they'll buy whatever you are selling in turn and that's the idea, isn't it?

The sixth rule – one which in almost every way must accompany you throughout your entire Network Marketing experience – is maintaining a strong sense of humor.

Invariably, you will run into a number of setbacks and disappointments along the way. You must retain the ability to sit back and smile away these bitter ashes, and out of them, build an even stronger resolve to continue on. I remember a certain axiom I learned when I was a kid in school, which sums it up most succinctly. And that axiom is this: "Nothing worthwhile ever comes easily." That's the truth my friends. You must be prepared for the bad times as well as the good, but if you can laugh off these heartaches and put them in their proper perspective, then nothing will be discouraging enough to stop you from picking up the pieces and starting over again with your optimism and faith intact. And as long as you hold tight to that ability to "let a smile be your umbrella on a rainy, rainy day," then eventually whatever it is you're striving for will happen for you.

Carol and I have never been pessimists. No matter what happened to us through the years, we never allowed it to interfere with our belief that some day all our dreams would come true through Network Marketing.

These then are what I consider to be the basic rules to your success in Network Marketing. They are not complicated ones, but they do take a strong dedication to live by and to use as the tools for building your personal land of milk and honey.

Once again let me stress that all of this is predicated by your present attitude toward yourself and the world you walk through.

Carol and I have often talked about what has happened to us these past eight years in Network Marketing and why it is we have achieved our success – and we've come to agree the most important reason for it is, we've never once lost our ability to dream.

We've never been cynical or jaded and all our lives we truly believed in ourselves. We were totally convinced that if we tried hard enough and were willing to work for it, there was nothing we couldn't eventually have. Our biggest problem was finding the means to that end. For us and I'm positive of this, for a great number of you who are reading this book, the vehicle is Network Marketing. It's the one system I know of that has no prerequisites for success. There are no deterrent factors to hinder it, either. No matter what your age, education, ethnic background, past business success or failure: none of these things matter as far as Network Marketing is concerned. What does matter, as I've mentioned so often throughout this book, is your personal need for all your fantasies to become reality with the freedom and time to enjoy them. There are no further requirements necessary other than an all-consuming desire to make your fondest dreams come true. This one factor is what will spell your success or failure within the Network Marketing system. As a ballplayer of the not too distant past so eloquently put it, "You've got to believe." And if you do believe and are willing to apply in every sense of the word the rules I listed as guidelines for you, then there is no one and nothing to prevent you from achieving what Carol and I have done.

Go for it and we'll see you on the beaches of the world

NOTES

NOTES

NOTES

NOTES

NOTES